Praise for *The Cave*

Ryan Vine's *The Cave* is a book of earthly wonders—from the electric squeeze of a young daughter's tiny hand; to the grizzled old father bathing himself with an air hose at the end of his shift; to "that rigid, old fuck, / the red oak, mid-/ winter, clutching / its leaves in the wind." These are poems that don't let go, by a poet who sings of human love with grit and honesty and extraordinary tenderness.

—PATRICK PHILLIPS, author of *Elegy for a Broken Machine* and *Song of the Closing Doors*

While the poems in *The Cave* are thoroughly contemporary, many of their philosophical underpinnings are as old as humanity itself. Vine's haunting meditations on fatherhood, for example, are as profound and enduring as any I've ever read. This is manly work, utterly masterful, and deeply moving.

—CONNIE WANEK, author of *Rival Gardens* and *On Speaking Terms*

The Cave is an unforgettable contribution to the poetry of paterfamilias written from deep inside "love's austere and lonely offices," as Robert Hayden put it. These poems are as indelible as scars—and just as full of ancient wisdom. Wonders abound: the cloud inside a dog's eye, the way a lake holds up the sky. Ryan Vine's poetry gives me that fully alive feeling, up to my neck in something I don't quite know how to swim and am glad for.

—DOBBY GIBSON, author of *Hold Everything* and *It Becomes You*

Ryan Vine enters into *The Cave* to mine the poetry of fatherhood, of childhood, to dip his cup into the underground river where those twinned currents meet and mingle their wisdom and unknowing. These open-hearted poems are crafty and beautifully crafted, vessels forged of swerving enjambment, sly slant rhyme, flickering illusions of endless imagination and mythic resonance—even Homer's cache of epic similes is plundered—all to hold the ache and tenderness of what can't be held: the hope and fear in trying to teach our kids to see what waits beyond the horizon when we can't see it ourselves, of living in a world where everything we love will disappear.

—MICHAEL BAZZETT, author of *The Echo Chamber* and *The Interrogation*

There is precision in these poems, and clarity and emotional intelligence. Beautiful writing.

—ILYA KAMINSKI, author of *Deaf Republic* and *Dancing in Odessa*

The Cave is a collection of poems that serve as a poet's time stamp in living. Ryan Vine divides his poetic findings into three sections, and in turn, the reader bears witness to the writer's becoming through him looking back at moving images and memories to look forward at what miracle is possible with finite time. Vine writes: *"I can't tell you / what I can hear. Maybe someone / else's memory, maybe suffering / muffled. I don't trust myself"* and we are transported to the moment one surrenders to the messy act of re-memory. The themes tumble from mortality and lust, to child-rearing and the divine mundane miracle of our living. Vine has a precise way of using language to discover one's capacity for love, desire, loss, rebirth, and one's search for joy.

—MAHAGONY BROWNE, author of *Chrome Valley* and *Vinyl Moon*

The poems of Ryan Vine shimmer from the tension between tenderness and toughness. This poet is not just messing around with words. The poems are compact, driven, urgent. They've got questions, and the main one seems to be Where's the place for love and wonder in a world so harsh and mean? Vine writes the kind of poem that haunts, that calls you back repeatedly. And that's, at last, the highest test for poetry.

—BART SUTTER, author of *Cotton Grass: New* and *Selected Poems of the North*

The Cave

ALSO BY RYAN VINE

Distant Engines

To Keep Him Hidden

WARD

The Cave

Poems

Ryan Vine

21st Century Poets, No. 41

★trp

TRP: The University Press of SHSU
Huntsville, Texas 77341

Library of Congress Cataloging-in-Publication Data

Names: Vine, Ryan, author.
Title: The cave : poems / Ryan Vine.
Other titles: Cave (Compilation)
Identifiers: LCCN 2025018796 (print) | LCCN 2025018797 (ebook) | ISBN 9781680034349 (trade paperback) | ISBN 9781680034356 (ebook)
Subjects: LCSH: Fatherhood--Poetry. | LCGFT: Poetry.
Classification: LCC PS3622.I545 C38 2025 (print) | LCC PS3622.I545 (ebook) | DDC 811/.6--dc23/eng/20250615
LC record available at https://lccn.loc.gov/2025018796
LC ebook record available at https://lccn.loc.gov/2025018797

FIRST EDITION

Cover art by istockpphoto | seregam
Author photo by Shawna Vine Photography

Cover design by Cody Gates, Happenstance Type-O-Rama
Interior design by Maureen Forys, Happenstance Type-O-Rama

Printed and bound in the United States of America
First Edition Copyright: 2025

TRP: The University Press of SHSU
Huntsville, Texas 77341
texasreviewpress.org

For Shawna, Leo and Aili

Contents

I

I wish at least I had some happy man
as father, growing old in this house.

—HOMER

Tick Check

I try to catch each kid
coming out of the shower.

That way I don't feel like a prison
guard, ordering them to strip

and spin: *Arms above your head.*
Now grab your bits and lift.

I once showed Leo and Aili a photo
of meth mouth to get a warning

about tooth brushing through.
I raised the tablet, and they ran

screaming down the dark hall,
the poor woman's face a light

in my hand, a crumbly hole.
What kind of father am I?

I'm trying to be here in these
long moments where nothing

happens but window smudges
soaked with sun. Then comes

the wet oration, the curtain
flung, Leo's towel tossed

back like a royal mantle.
And now I'm on the toilet,

splitting Aili's damp hair
into rows, down which I work

to keep my attention and not
float away again to become

like an alien, high above
a foreign world, afraid

to find the life I'm looking for.

I'm So Lonely and I Just Love You

my son sang, over and over,
his back to me, as he plucked
a tune on his tiny guitar,
except he can't play—
he's only five—so I
must have been dreaming,
but Pessoa's ghost told me
once in a dream—"we are
two abysses—a well
staring at the sky."
                              Leo sang
beautifully and in a way
that gave his repeated
lines a kind of lyric
completion, like twelve
good bars of blues.
The guitar was tiny
but big for him, so
he stood behind it,
singing, *I'm so lonely*
and I just love you.
I said, *I'm right here*
to his back. *I'm so*
lonely, he sang.
I understand, I said,
and tried to walk
around to see his face,
but he kept turning
away.
          I remember
I said, but the words
I knew, the words
from books that worked

for me, were for him
like fat, white streaks
in puddles: worms
the day after rain.
I'm so lonely, he sang.

Tischer Creek

It's hot, so I haul the kids
and two of their friends, brothers,
to our favorite swimming hole.
There's an easy waterfall
with a spot for my butt thousands
of years of flow have worn smooth,
where the cool water washes
over my swollen knee, and a sheer
rock face like a slide, down which
all four kids plunge again and again.
At first, they're flying, they're birds
hunting fish, they're clouds
crashing into their own reflections;
but play changes quickly, and already
the Titanic is sinking and fast. *Look,*
one brother says, *tentacles! A whirlpool,*
the other shouts. *The Kraken!* So out
come the harpoons, which they pitch
into the water, screaming and tearing
at the air as they go down. Soon,
they start at each other, pantomiming
blood squirting from their necks, hearts
exploding like bombs. My daughter
yells *help, help,* and practices floating
face down in the creek, in the shade
and sun, where the boys above her
laugh and die, laugh and die.

Lego Motorcycle

I tell her it's time,
and 5-year-old Aili

lifts the tiny, blue bike,
stares into it and says

she's leaving tomorrow
on a long journey,

and in this new town
there are no rules.

Trying to Teach My Kids to See Them Coming When I Can't See Them Myself

Take this respected professor
and chair of history at the College
of St. Watchamacallit. You know
the type—still waiting for word
from Harvard on the day
he retires. He stepped to the urinal
next to me once and announced
to the wall we were staring at,
that as for him he'd *decided—*
years ago—to live the life
of the mind. We thought
he was harmless, his doorway
lean, his endless talking
shit like, *yes, but were the Germans*
culpable, as though we weren't
wading through our fat, white
1990s American lives high
on culpability.
                    Now I'm at this
party years later, sneaking
a smoke on the deck, when
I recognize him and his wife
leaving a house across the street.
He gets in his car first, closest
to the door, then she in hers,
an older model parked behind.
His car starts immediately. Hers
turns a few times, but before
the engine fires, he honks,
and I hear a clunk, which I think
comes from her car dropping

into reverse, but I see he's
pushed his bumper into hers.
He pulls forward a few feet
and backs into her car again,
which is presumably also
his car, just keeps crashing into it,
as she tries to get the engine going,
as it turns and turns but doesn't catch.
He smashes her car so hard it slides
sideways over the sidewalk and curb:
wheels screeching, plastic bumper
cracked, hood buckled, streak of black
mud through the manicured grass.

So she sits, 10 & 2, staring at him,
as he gets out and turns and looks
at me, and rises—floating—slowly
above both cars, lifted by the billowing
smoke beneath his waving black cape,
so the whole block can clearly see
(Look! I knew it!): a Sith Lord,
a super criminal, or just some royal
piece of fucking shit! Except
he doesn't. He won't. He stays
in his seat, adjusts his rear-view
mirror, lifts a tiny, sharp flame
to his cigarette, quietly rolls
down the window, waves
to her, and in his mysteriously
unmarked car drives
slowly down the street.

Obstinate Optimist

Like the sumac lifting
its burning dark

candles all winter;
like the bright crab

apple's bloody stains
in the perfect

snow; like that
rigid, old fuck,

the red oak, mid-
winter, clutching

its leaves in the wind—
I don't let go.

United Martial Arts

Stoic, sweet but severe, the Greens
facing class perform horse stance
and double punch and a number
of other useless moves in a street fight,
but the roomful of kids is happy,
striking at the air, watching
themselves in the floor-
to-ceiling mirror vanquish
imagined enemies. I've been trying
to teach kindness as a keel, and now
knife strike is a daily move in our house.
We swat at ghost assailants, chop
open doors, say, you'd better stop
right there, our hands flat as plates.
Quickness is key, to be quick
as the closing door slices sound
to silence. Every Wednesday,
Leo and Aili in bleached-white gis
bounce down the stairs, swinging
above their heads the wrinkled belts
happily to the car. My favorite
backseat faces: their constant
changing revises all expectations
I have of beauty and permanence,
when the bright features don't blind me.
It's a big class tonight. The Greens
are busy. Leo's running blocking drills;
Aili's practicing her ki ai; and I,
on my usual corner seat, half-
reading, half-watching, learn now
how important grasping block
really is, as they both run over

on break to demonstrate the move
you'd use to grab the loose gi
of the enemy you can't see—
only feel—as he rushes by.

40 Below

While others are out
tossing boiling water

into the air, we stay inside
and watch lemon bits

float through hot whiskeys
like a slow snowfall.

I left a pile of sunflower
seeds on the sidewalk, a bright

carrot on the stoop.
For the crows, I threw out

something sweet: eaves
from a gingerbread roof

no one's going to eat.
It's only 4:30, but already

it's dark, and Lake Superior's
sea smoke's risen

like a white wall
come to close us in.

But we're not worried.
We've seen this before.

In the cold dark, we know
to survive we need

to help each other; we know
pride is useless as a fireplace.

Open the flue, and winter
sticks its fingers in, stirring us

like a drink. Frost seeps through
and climbs the bedroom wall,

the vegetable oil in the corner
cupboard clouds and freezes,

and when the house pops
like someone's thrown

a snowball at the siding,
you'll find no one there

but snowbanks, stuck, solid,
halfway up the chain-link fence

like slow, stupid thieves.
Still, we're relieved

every time we hear—
in the quiet basement,

in the damp bluestone
corner, where the wolf

spiders wait in tiny white
caves hung like shelves—

the old furnace whine and kick
like a haunted drum set.

We march up the stairs
wearing our blankets.

We sleep to the wonky beat.

Preschool

We're walking to the car, crunching snow
across the yard, overburdened, as usual

with backpacks and books and lunches
in bags, when my son says, *You*

would make a good grave. What? I say.
My gun could do that. You don't have a gun,

I remind him, as he climbs into his car seat
and waits, smiling, for the familiar zip

and click of the belt. *Dad,* he says, staring
down the fingergun inches from my face,

you're my best friend. Across the street,
the birch look thinner and whiter in snow.

I turn off the news, but too late—too late—
and drive slowly so we can watch two crows

tuck and shoot through the tangled branches,
like the two he loves from his favorite

storybook, Odin's black angels, Hugin and Munin,
thought and memory, sent out across

the world each morning with the hope
that they come back. Today, luckily, we

unbuckle his seatbelt, and my son kisses
my hand before we cross the street.

Today we hang his coat on the hook
by his name, and he runs through

the open door and into the bright room
of children playing without saying goodbye.

Lake Erie in Light Rain

We've waded to our necks
after another long day in the car
headed east, our minds

on the Atlantic. The orange
skies of the Greenwood fire
are behind us now, the record-

breaking heat—inhospitable
as this Interstate—and our prayers
we left scattered in the air

as we passed a few of the new
American monuments: Floyd
Square, Kenosha, Island Park.

We're dusty, tired and trying
to get away—who can blame us—
when we decide here is good

enough for today. I hold my breath
and leave the others behind,
wade out eye-deep, let the water

fill my ears, but I can't tell you
what I can hear. Maybe someone
else's memory, maybe suffering

muffled. I don't trust myself.
These are the easy figures
I've been given: to feel held,

by the Great Lake, that Erie
will somehow heal us. I mean, it is
holding up the sky. The calm

water's even hopping back
out to meet the falling rain.
I go under, open my eyes.

Down here in the cold green
I used to believe that we went on
and on. I try to go deeper, to sink

into the shifting waves of sand,
but I can't. I turn and see
Shawna, Leo and Aili: three

beheaded bodies floating like ghosts.

Eating the Kids

Uvalde, Texas May 24, 2022

We don't realize
what we're doing,
my wife and I,
when we choose—
she, our daughter,
and I, our son—
but soon we're rolling
up their sleeves
to get to the tenderer
meat. We'd already
sat down to dinner, so
the kids don't notice
or pretend not to.
It doesn't matter.
They do what we say.
If they survive, they'll do
what we do. Their tiny
bones break like fish
bones on the plate.
I'm nearly to the neck
when I see my wife's
already finished.
Such a fast eater!
The good dogs wait
beneath the table, as we
motion with our empty
glasses for another
round, but we're alone.
We look up, astonished.
The kids are gone.
We weren't even hungry.

The Cave

Leo and Aili hover above me,
playing doctor. Apparently,

I've been shot through the eyes
by a man hunting deer. Your eyes

are ruined, they say and lay
a pair of wool socks over my face,

over the fact that I just got in
late last night from a week's vacation,

still a little drunk, skin pink with sun.
In Plato's allegory, the ignorant ones

kill the traveler for what he's seen,
but here—on the kitchen floor—they feel

for my pulse with a Styrofoam stethoscope,
take a rusted tuning fork to my bad elbow.

He's really sick, my daughter says and leans
down to blow her syrupy

breath into me. *Agreed,*
says my son and taps a finger to my cheek.

For a moment, they're silent, as shadows
like magnificent frigate birds soar

across the socks on my face, until—at
last—around my wrists they clamp

the iron bonds and drag the chains
jingling through the dirt. Like a pang

of a sweet too sweet: the sound
of their spike driven deep into stone.

II

If someone is sensible he would remember that
the two disturbances in the eyes arise from two sources:
by changing from the light to darkness or darkness into light.

—PLATO

Air Hose

In the back of the Body Shop,
beside the banging air compressor,
past the ten-foot pig stove
into which we rolled old railroad ties
to burn overnight, my father
is blowing himself clean again.
It's how he closed the door
every day on the day's work.
He's on the other side now
of the row of cars half-finished
and just begun, and he's tired,
lifting the shiny thumb-lever grip
to his head, starting at the top,
where the compressed air
like water from a garden hose
rolls over his hair,
and when he brings the bright
nozzle to his chin and looks to the ceiling,
his bangs fling up as though he's falling.
He moves the hose side to side,
quickly over his torso,
pasting the shirt against
his big, hard belly, then flag-
poles his skinny legs to spend
good, long seconds on his brown,
paint-stained boots.
I've grieved his leaving
too many times.
I'm not going to do it again.
I am my own father

was a lie I'd learned to announce
        as he stood in the back
                the last one there
                        blowing off the poison dust
                every weeknight before he left
        the Body Shop for Bridges Bar
then came home.

Tao of Jeet Kun Do

Books are a load of crap.
—PHILIP LARKIN

I learned to punch by reading
Bruce Lee. I'd already spent years
inches from the screen wishing
I was him, his airborne body
slicing the room in half, but I
was chubby and slow and worried
about how—exactly—things
are done, so I got my nose
in a book.
Plant your front foot
at a 45 toward the target, lead
with your strongest arm, let the punch
originate from the ground, through
the hips like a whip, and imagine
and aim for a space opening six inches
past the chin.
Only a few days after
I'd finished *The Tao of Jeet Kun Do,*
a boy at a kegger beneath
the Fond Du Lac bridge
told my girlfriend, *shut up bitch.*
I said, *hey man, you can't say that.*
And he said, *fuck you AND that bitch*
and walked very slowly toward me
with his fists raised, just slow
enough that I could plant my front
foot, turn and see that place
six inches past his chin,
and then

beyond that behind him
like a backdrop I can't shake,
the tiny opening widens
exponentially—big-
bang quick—like a dark,
endless vista, and in it he falls
back again through the long grass,
and I'm down on him, straddling
his body like a board, screaming
inches from his face. His eyes
are fluttering moths. His mouth
moves like he's still talking,
but there's a hole in the blood
where his tooth should be.

St. Margaret Mary's, Morgan Park, 1987

My mother locked her crooked
broken pinkie over mine

on the pew back in front of us
while Jesus from the crucifix

looked down on his emissary
who looked down from the altar

at Billy D.Z. in the front pew
who'd turned around to face

the congregation and though
he was from the neighborhood

he was Italian and self-made so he
looked down on us, but we knew

in our blood that rich was a thing
we would be someday if we just

worked hard enough and prayed
and gave to Billy and the Father

and the Good Lord Jesus Christ.

Duluth

We tried to forget last winter
before it was over; we closed
our eyes, and more snow fell.

Even on the sunny days: white
flakes floating by. Fuck this
place, we said and mainlined

cheap pizza, murdered boxes
of wine. Remember that night
the wind slapped smoke back

down the chimney, and a black
cloud roared through our bedroom
like a bear? We burst into the yard

coughing, blasted, in our underwear.
The neighbors think we're nuts.
Snowy decades pass, and still

we're hopping back and forth—
foot to foot—our glowing pink
skin parka-thick, taking turns

at the frozen channel, chopping ice
with this stick, trying to get the fucking
sliding glass door fucking shut.

Kestrels

All day the down fell,
	fat and white
like slow, wet snow.
	And dark feathers—
like maple seeds, shook—
	spun in columns
of warm summer air, as we
	sat beneath with bloodies
and snits—our cheese,
	chips, and deviled eggs.
We counted six perched
	in the huge red pines,
dropping cones as they moved,
	dropping shit, too,
which opened occasionally
	in the wind like small,
white plastic bags.
	But when the headless
carcasses started falling
	(blue jay, finch, robin—
they hadn't even eaten it!)
	we thought, what monsters!,
sipping our vodka. What waste!
	We agreed: something
had to be done, so my father
	got his shotgun
and turned one into a red
	puffy mess of feathers.
Another, he beheaded,
	and she fell to our feet
just like her victims.
	Old sure shot sat back

down and drained his drink,
          and we laughed, as usual,
not knowing what else to do.
          The rest of the kestrels
were unmoved, kept on
          killing, and we pretended
not to notice the feathers
          fall, not to feel
the down rising on our shoulders.
          We raised our glasses
as though we'd won, asked
          for another and stared
through the squall
          at the sun rippling
across Lake Nebagamon
          like a loose
layer of Saran Wrap.

Spanish Songs

It was only me and one other kid
who showed that first day
for the two-credit language lab
in musty Tower Hall.

He didn't last long, poor kid,
by the second week gone,
and who knows if he ever
shook his fear of other people
the wide Midwest lays in our brains
as a painful silence.
                                        I stayed
because I was afraid,
and I knew if I ran
from Sister Mary and her
singing, well, everyone knows
the rest.
                                        O
sister Mary, so puffy
and cute in what I remember
as a dress like a burlap sack,
and as she sang Guantanamera
and plucked the plastic strings
on her ratty old Fender,
I slowly learned to sing along.

Twice that semester
before a vocab quiz,
                                        lovely
sister Mary—who knew
I wouldn't pass, who must have
smelled the stale alcohol, sensed
the shame, which also

has a kind of smell, over-
whelming all else, like
dog shit on a shoe—
sweet sister Mary stared
into my squinty, blood-shot eyes,
and stood and left the room.

And I won't say here
if I cheated, but I passed,
and at the end of the semester
when we hugged and laughed
and I whispered I'll miss you,
I meant it.
Sister Mary,
you should know: still,
when the day stretches on
like a lecture, when my fear
and cinderblock sadness
threaten to bed me down
or worse, I sing guantanemara,
guajira guantanamera,
and try to stay,
so I'm here
for the next song.

Sex Tape

Maybe y'all've seen it,
that lame insurance commercial

about the guy who—now
an old man—visits scenes

from his youth as an annoying
ghost and whispers

into his own young ear, *no, please,*
don't do it. Get off the gunnel.

Put down that rope swing. Well,
now I'm the kill-joy ghost

in our illegal basement apartment
in Boston where my ex-girlfriend

and I shot this shaky footage.
I'm the white, old face attached

to yet another bright screen,
as younger bodies travel through it.

I'd been cleaning when I came across
this dusty cassette and now

I'm having a hard time believing
we were so beautiful, our long limbs

honed and shiny, though we mostly
hated ourselves and so each other.

There's the usual stuff, I guess:
what you'd expect to find

on a sex tape. In our studio
apartment, at the end of the dark

hallway of discarded appliances—
the stairway light blinking,

only one way in or out, bars
over the window to the alley

where the girl who lived above us
parked her bright, blue Audi—

where the silverfish and house
centipedes brushed by our bare feet—

we always found a reason to fuck.
And now I've turned the camera

on myself, so there's a face, mine
but not, filling the screen and on

the screen, staring back, so close
we could kiss, and I'm saying, no,

don't kiss her. I'm saying to my face
on the screen: don't put your hand

up under her dress. She plans
to leave you for the rich man

whose dad owns the paint shop
down the block. Hers is a future

of rooftop parties on Newberry Street,
floating with turtles off of Cape Cod.

Next year, she'll have his child.
This leaving will take months

of lies and fighting, half-truths
and denial, paranoia so bad

you'll come to in the Common
one sunny afternoon of tourists

and swan boats and make way
for ducklings and realize

that even though you've stolen
her phone, you'll never get into it.

Of the 10,000 possible combinations
what you thought was your love

is not one of them. Now a thief,
you'll lie back in the grass

and cry, like I'm crying now,
saying no, don't, but I can't

hear myself, as she moves
to take my hand and leads us—

naked—away from standing
in the mirror, across the one

room slowly to the futon
covered in clothes.

Lake Superior Scenic Railroad

I didn't memorize the list of facts
a train-car long and hung over
recite them through the sour
microphone so sleepy tourists
could bob their heads on the early-

morning Saturday run, but here I am
again, competing
with the rhythm of the tracks:
To your right is the mighty
Lake Superior, and like many gods

it goes by many names: The Inland Sea,
The North Coast, The Sweetwater Sea,
as folks from here like to call it,
or the Gichi-Gami, which comes
from the Chippewa and translates roughly

to the long-shining waters.
You know what else translates roughly?
Chippewa. There is no
such people. That word comes
from the dead ear of a French imperialist,

a mis-interpretation of the pronunciation
of Ojibwa. (The conductor
pantomimes slitting his own throat.)
But, hey, that's a whole other train ride.
Through the window you may feel

Lake Superior's endlessness
reaching into you to stroke a longing
in the water of your own body,
and that's because she's 31,700 square miles
with more shoreline than the state

of California. Or for you geographically-
inclined: that's the combined areas
of Vermont, Massachusetts, Rhode
Island, Connecticut, New Jersey
and New Hampshire. Let's face it:

she's bigger than most of the East Coast
and much more interesting.
Can you imagine being responsible
for 10% of the world's fresh water,
3 quadrillion gallons of it? Well, Lake Superior

wakes every morning with that fact,
enough to flood all of North and South
America in one foot,
and still every night fights off
nightmare Monsanto and Nestle,

and all the other toothy, thirsty
transnationals. (Again,
the conductor.)
Let me put it this way: this lake
has an island with a lake with an island

with a lake. At her deepest point
she's 1,333 feet. And the waves?
The largest ever recorded
rose 51 feet in Whitefish Bay.
It should be no surprise then to hear

of the 350 recorded shipwrecks and the countless
men who went down with them.
No light.
No bacteria. 38 degrees
Fahrenheit on average. Sailors down there

like they were on the day they died.
But the fact that sinks me
like a boat: the sun
rises on Lake Superior's
Western shore a full 35 minutes later

than when it rose in the east. Contemplate
that curve! Stare for as long as you'd like.
There are few days
you'll love more than those you spend
wandering the rocky beaches, stopping

to sit in the sand beside a grove of red pine.
In the Russian Orthodox Church,
they say if you pray hard
enough while staring into the face
of an icon a lake will appear into which

you'll fall and find your soul.
But we know that's wrong—we
who stumble from the platform,
or still in the vestibule staring,
some of us already down on the beach, stunned

by the smooth, blue-white surface, haunted
        by the hunched, green boulders hundreds
                of feet below. Lake Superior
        pulls our burning faces from us to float
like prayers, as the only soul—the one soul—

appears, long-shining, in whom we happily drown.

There's a Poem in That

a good friend tells me
(innocently, honestly;
she wants me to find
a place for it, meaning
for this experience) after
I describe the dead wolf
hanging by her hind legs
from a ceiling joist
in my in-law's garage.
See, they had sent me
for more beer knowing
the sight of this month's trap
would make me sick:
a pine marten, a badger,
two coyotes too, all stiff
and upside down.
But the wolf was huge.
She had her own joist
and it bowed low.
I'd shoved opened
the stuck back door, flipped
the light and jumped: her
face inches from mine.
Her eyes were open.
Frozen blood had stiffened
the fur around her mouth.
Fifteen thousand years ago
bones of the *Canis lupus*
began to appear in human
graves. Some archeological
studies suggest as far back
as thirty-five. We do this

to ourselves. I crack the beer
I came to get and watch
my hot breath rise
into the rafters. She tried
to chew her leg off. The sun
squeezes through a dirty
window, cutting the frozen
air, illuminating the immaculate
snowmobile. I've tried
to be like a clam given
grains of sand. I can't
do it anymore. What's inside
for dinner, I wonder.
Panfuls of mushy fish?
A side of malicious whispers?
I'm nearly in tears. What
makes a poem a poem?
What meaning can we find?
Isn't this just another story
I'm telling myself, hoping
what happened will change
in the telling? I need to stand
awhile, wait for my eyes to dry.
I won't let them see me like this.

Hangover, Sunday, 8 AM

and through the hotel lobby comes this girl,
she could be ten, she could be twelve (who cares),
her hair still wet from her morning swim;
it's turned her red shirt redder in two blotches
on her shoulders and chest, and she's pushing
this luggage dolly—an empty luggage dolly—
one of its wheels missing, so the other
three scrape and squeal and catch, as she
pushes it across the milky tile, across the golden-
swirled carpet with importance—slowly
she pushes it—her face scrunched in the careful
consideration of a ten-year-old bent to a serious task,
her plastic flip-flops squeaking in her-
foot-sized puddles, across the whole fucking lobby,
then bangs it into the hallway wall, because
the missing wheel throws her occasionally
out of control, so she leans back and jerks
it toward her and pushes it forward again
but harder. Now, she's slamming it into other
luggage dollies, trying to stuff it into the small
room where they store the luggage dollies,
and coatless hangers clatter to the floor,
like spent shells, and some huge cannon,
some wide, dark mouth has spit you out right here.

What Is This That Makes This My Life

It started as a white point
to the left of his right iris.

When he remembered,
he'd check on it, trying

to focus his good eye
on the stretching.

It was like a needle
about to push through

from inside his eyeball.
Like in the movies,

he thought, this will
eventually, in the course

of my otherwise
mundane life,

become a kind of sad,
red claw stretching

over my eye as an ever-
expanding net, and I—

I—my preferred pronoun,
this weak-ass pillar,

tiniest and slowest
of space and pace

between planes—I
will slowly be consumed.

Fine, he said to the stinky, caked
toothbrushes in the glass,

fine to the running
water in the sink,

to the drain
tinkling, but before

that day, before he goes
down there with that,

he will live his life
like the tiny totem

of terrified faces
every American

electrical outlet is:
two long and silent

screams.

Sea Glass

In which the receding sea makes Black Beach a mirror
and I'm given another sky, where the green

glass like a lozenge floats—rubbed rough and soft—
and I feel after a long month of worry

        the sea

reminding the shard: you're sand. I roll the glass clean
between my hands, dip it into a tidal pool and hold it up

for the sun's simple refrain to fill: you can't stay
sharp; I'm the light. So the less and less

I hold each morning I work to revise, and revision
is the place I plan to spend my days. There's no such thing

        as done.

III

Who shall say I am not
the happy genius of my household?

—WILLIAM CARLOS WILLIAMS

In the Clearing

Leo steps from the woods
his tight blond curls lit
from behind by the sun
the aspen pollen falling
slowly and puffy and white
like it's still snowing
in the middle of June.
Now the day's gone
and we're following fireflies
into the lake and the moon
lights the rippling water
around his little legs *the moon*
he says joyously the moon
is peeking through the trees
like a man with a flashlight
looking for something lost
for years in the bottom
of a boozy bag and I feel
that I'm finally found.

Doing the Dishes

Google-less and lacking
Siri's assistance, I ask my dog
Stella questions like, *Hey Stella,*
how high is Mount Everest?

And she wakes and lifts her head
and stares at me, as I turn to look
at what's recently like a dim glow
in each pupil—like candlelight

coming from another room—
and for a moment our ignorance
rises together like an aroma
in this room, fills it, seeps through

the window screens, wraps around
the roof, tapers and is on approach
to that stark, snowy altitude
above which the blue is nearly white.

She's right, of course, Stella,
as she sighs and lies back down,
so I rappel and shake the soap
from my hands to lie down

next to her, to push my face
into her matted fur—avoiding
the painful tumors—and to ask
quietly a question she can't hear.

Sugar Bush

There's no better smell
        than steam from the boiling
sap in the lopsided shack.
        Like Pepe Le Pews, we float
through the trees, inches
        above the muddy tractor tracks.
I mean our feet are clean, man,
        as we enter this altar
deep in the woods and pray
        through our nostrils and place
on our tongues wafers of warm
        maple candy Aunty Leddie
loves to make. We do it
        in remembrance of the trees,
clear blood of a covenant older
        than *the* covenant,
and the stinging sweetness enters
        our bodies and god
damn if we aren't saved.
        Sitting the sugar shack
overnight—attending
        the bubbling sap's
swirling white rise above
        the long aluminum pan—
we don't mind, because
        nighttime isn't nighttime
when you're dry as a cotton
        candy cone in a spinning,
sugary cloud. And the moon
        in the window, not the bright
one in the sky, but the dim
        reflection in the glass

just to the side of the cold
rock in our eyes, becomes
a face clearer than *the* face,
a tiny confidant, a secret
lover who listens to our whispers and sees
that the Earth, even dark,
even after everything we've done,
is still so sweet.

Orange Sun Rising

The morning before
the milk goes sour
I taste the bales
strapped with sun,
smell the molasses
oats, see—when I lift
the glass to my lips—
the bright space between
the boards inflate,
as though the patient
bull, the barn cats and I
are all about to float away
in a big, luminous, wooden
balloon, and I'm not
just standing here
in my underwear, milk
in my mouth, staring
out the window in this
momentarily quiet kitchen
before today's tasks
come to spoil what
I think is my mind.

Youth Soccer

Like if you could take the quick
from quick silver, so it was just
a clump of slowly moving metal,
these kids move from one
side of the pitch to the other,
kicking at shins, so close
they could hug. Leo has no idea
what to do, but it's not his fault.
This team's had more games
than practices. Only the kids
whose dads are out after work
kicking around know what's going on.
I'm no help: skateboarder, fringe-
fucker, never played well
with others, spent too much time
staring at single things, waiting
for my vision to blur. I take off
my shoes and sink my bare feet
into the cool, perfectly manicured
grass. *Spread out,* my wife yells,
mark up, as the kids stand
together, as though holding hands,
waiting for a throw in, a blank-
faced, disinterested wall. Leo,
alone, behind them, stares
at the passing clouds, raises his arms
above his head and rises again
and again on his toes like he's
about to lift away, and someone
behind me screams—as another boy
breaks off, windmilling across
the pitch, bouncing as though chasing

an invisible rabbit—*No Guts*
No Glory! But isn't it No Guts
No Gory? I can never remember.
What I do remember: at their age
I would wipe my hand across fake
wood paneling, and the grain—
like swiping your hand through smoke—
twisted and slithered as though alive.

Crough Patrick

for Russell Gran, 1936–2017

I.

I climbed Ireland's holiest mountain to see
Clew Bay, Achill & Claire.

I stood at the spot where it's said
St. Patrick fasted for 40 days and nights

to steal from the Celts the myth
of the mountain in the same way

he'd go on to split their stone
suns with a cross. Legend is

the crows fucked with him
hard the whole time. Demon

crows, he called them, but we know
they're just crows.

II.

So I was surprised
having come for the view

to find you there, or you
but not you, as the stone

church at summit rose
like a whitehead, and the wind

nearly pushed me over.
Appeared isn't right

and as I sat down and tried
to write *appeared*

on my waterproof notepad
the wind and rain

wiped the shiny ink
across the paper,

so the word began
to run and streak,

disappearing even
before its meaning.

III.

Which came first, the crow
or the demon, the word

or the haunting,
the bleached church

stones, or the bright
void behind?

I'm told to believe
joy is the antidote,

that even a teaspoon
could send us spinning

through the days ahead.

IV.

We carried the same

sour tone, and blamed
dusty West Duluth.

We couldn't help
but taste it; the kicked

dirt just came up
every time we talked.

Maybe the height
I seek now, this spinning

at the top, isn't
to see, but to keep

inside like a gyroscope,
so I can stand against

whatever wind.

V.

I joked that a good life

was nothing but learning
to become a larger, more

joyful receptacle for pain,
and you laughed, already

fat and pulled your shirt up
over your impossibly

large belly to show me
the scar that ran

from your belt
to your throat.

VI.

Pain as a final companion
Pain as unconditional love

Pain as a silence in which there is no pain
before your father slapped your mother in the street

Pain as a green field six feet above which floats a blue balloon you chase
into the alley behind the house where your mother fucked the mailman

Pain as a hazy cloud and you're seated at the center
somehow in the West Duluth that is my West Duluth

fifty years later at the far end of which
our brothers are still men

we talk to

VII.

The night you died

I'd turned off my phone,
so when you called

I was sleeping
when your neighbor

heard you, when
the medics waited

outside your door,
while the manager jingled

through her ring of keys.
I was asleep as they tried

to resuscitate you,
and you died on the floor.

When I got to your apartment
the next morning

they'd already taken your body,
so I laid on the rug next to your bed

but couldn't look up.
I turned and saw the white

gauze soiled red, closed
my eyes and felt through

the ceiling a new, long, dark
hall stretching out.

IIX.

A sun-bleached stone church,
nearly night at the top

of a holy mountain:
a black halo of crows.

Like yours, my life
wasn't so much

ambition as it was
survival, which is why

I was always poeming
as you used to say,

Russ, poeming,
and now I'm afraid

of grief, so again,
I'm poeming

here at the desk,
poeming to you,

because how else
can I talk to you now?

IX.

The moon is out early.
Back in Minnesota

it's winter, the season
we spend our lives

preparing for, but here
there's no preparation

sufficient for this moon,
this breach the meteorite left

as it opened the Earth
and hung the hole

like a light in the sky.

Advice for the Apathetic

For many years I was content
composing the poem in my mind,

never committing it to paper.
On morning walks I'd uncover

a line, by lunch it'd turned to ten,
and when it was time to crawl

into bed, my poem crawled in
behind me, nearly perfect.

I closed my eyes,
and it shined, spinning

like a trophy on display.
When my mind loosened, sleep

washed the poem away.
In the shower, in the morning,

my eyes still closed, I watched it
spin again into bright fragments,

liquified, like Li Bai, who blind
drunk on wine and reaching

for the floating moon, fell
from the gunnel and broke

into a thousand poems unfolding.
My prayer those days: if I lose track

of time, may time lose track of me.
It didn't work that way, of course.

Those poems are gone now, and so am I.

Good Company

Walking through the snowy field
the day after
I walked through the snowy field,

I step next to my first set of prints
so anyone who cares to can see
I was never alone.

Stella

our poor, black dog
is dying. She's all
hips and ribs, her
breathing's thin too
and shallow, and
this morning—when
we tried our walk—
she stopped in the street
and looked at me, like
c'mon man. So today,
I'll bring her back
to the vet, where he'll
sedate her and inject
a barbiturate to stop
her heart. I've been here
before, this slowness
that comes first, so we'll
sit a minute in the sun
in the yard, and I'll stare
up at the blue spruce,
past the outer branches
and into where the bark
turns darker, and puddles
of bright lichen grow—
where the red-breasted
nuthatch hop-picks
at earwigs—and I'll tell Stella
the lie of a life I lived
before this one, when I woke
in the woods at a cliff,
and earwigs in waves covered
my body, climbing

like I was the tree, but I wasn't
afraid, because I stretched
to two points at the top
and down into the ground
like a trunk, and birds
swooped between my boughs
for the feast, and when I
remembered to look up
across the valley a river
wound into the horizon,
like the one she loved
to swim—though she never
was any good at it, mostly
thrashed to keep from sinking,
her head barely above
her splash—but this river
looked like it hung from the sky,
a flashing dog tail
of water that wagged light
from there to here
where we are now, even
at the vet, and even the vet
is crying, as I hold Stella's head,
and her tongue pokes out,
and her breathing stops,
and I've never noticed
until now how heavy
her head is.

Junk Drawer

Don't just go shoving your hand into it,
den of domesticity that it claims to be;

still some things can cut: the open
scissors, errant needles, the loose

thumb tacks like little assassins,
their small, golden hats hiding

the single thought. But if you're careful,
you can usually find what you need:

pencils, stickers, patch
for the backyard pool the kids pop

every summer. Eventually,
we started putting everything in there:

screwdriver, tape measure, bike parts,
pine cones, so the drawer's always

almost shut, notepads sticking out
like an underbite. Try to pull it open

and its scraping is November wind
off the big lake, caught in the ancient

blue spruce. And yet there's still room
for Petoskey stones, plans for the winter

fort, curled school photos, the whole
flashing harbor, horns from the passing

lakers, the long, bright trails they cut
like slugs over a sidewalk, and I swear

I just heard my children as they were
years ago, Leo and Aili, running home

from the bus, impatient to play,
planning out the next scene of a life-

long game before they filled
the backyard with their squabbling

and laughter. It's a wonder
this thing closes at all.

The Great Journey

—for Mike Bazzett

He told his wife all his worries
were falling away: the job, which now
only occasionally caused him sleeplessness;
the illness; the chronic pain; the childhood
like a wet coat he wore everywhere.
All of it, he said, he could feel
falling away from him each morning
as he crossed the yard to work
in the small room he had built
in the garage with his father. Each day
he arrived less and less what he thought
himself to be. One day, he imagined,
he would disappear completely,
as he stood looking out the window,
in the corner of which the red squirrels
had chewed a small hole. Finally, he saw
himself the size of an acorn; how easily
he could roll through this opening and out
into the yard, and from there who knows?
Maybe something big. Maybe something small.

Aili Leads Me into the Woods

to a place across the street she wants to show me
to the hollow beneath the grove of squeaky willow
to a crick in the creek she's cleared of snow
to the spot she was standing when she first saw
the deer melt on the hillside, three
bright green portals to sunnier days
where a mama—I try to explain—
and two fawns must have spent the snowy night
but before I can finish she grabs my hand
and squeezes and for most of my life
I've wanted language always
to accompany me but for right now I'm good.

Afterword

Plato's "Allegory of the Cave" mesmerized me as a young reader. I remember imagining myself there at the rock, wondering what my chains might be, then wondering—almost simultaneously—is that me between the fire and the wall, a fool trying to fool someone, or am I slowly making my way up to the bright air and sun? I'm still inspired by its power, both as a metaphor and as an instructive tool, and the allegory has helped me understand, at various stages of my evolution, where I am in the process, and where the people are—and who they are—around me.

Fatherhood, particularly in the first few years, feels a bit like descending into a cave too; in here—sleepy with the shadows—it's easy to forget. Of course, Shawna and Leo and Aili are near—the love and joy almost its own light—but friends disappear, the outside world dims, and what I understood to be the life I was living suddenly wasn't that life anymore.

And because the allegory is a constant preoccupation, it occurred to me as I was deep in this book to use it as a guiding metaphor for the way in which I organized the poems. Ignorance to knowledge, knowledge to ignorance—this life-long tug of war with the self, this ascending and descending—is the stuff of poetry.

Which is why I wanted to include Plato's allegory in my book: to pay homage to the man who would bar me from his republic, to give Homer the first voice in my cave, and to share with you what's meant so much to me. If you haven't read it before, welcome to Plato's cave. If you have, I hope you find something new in this new translation of the 2400-year-old allegory by my friend and colleague, Dr. Drew Mannatter.

I'll meet you above, the trees bursting with sunlight.

—RYAN VINE

Plato
The Allegory of the Cave

Translated by Drew Mannatter, Ph.D.

SOCRATES: Compare, then, our condition in regards to education and its lack to such a scenario as the following. First, imagine a sort of dwelling in an underground cave, which has a long entrance open toward a light. Here, men live, with their legs and necks fettered by chains, so that they have to remain motionless and only look forward, since the fetters prevent the movement of their bodies. Above and behind them, and at a distance, the light from a fire is glowing. Between the fire and the prisoners there is a road, along which a wall is built up, just as low screens are set by puppeteers where they display their show.

GLAUKON: I can see all that.

SOCRATES: Also see, then, men carrying along this wall props of all sorts made of stone and wood and other materials, which cast images of men and other animals, and very likely some of those bearing the equipment would be speaking while others would be silent.

GLAUKON: You are describing a strange image and strange prisoners.

SOCRATES: Like to us. For first, do you think that such prisoners would see anything of themselves or each other except the shadows that are projected onto the wall of the cave in front of them?

GLAUKON: How could they? If throughout their life they were forced to hold their heads motionless?

SOCRATES: What of the things being carried behind them? Is this case not the same?

GLAUKON: Of course.

SOCRATES: If, then, they were able to converse with one another, do you not think that they would mistakenly equate the passing objects with the images they saw?

GLAUKON: Of course.

SOCRATES: And what then? If the prison had an echo, do you think that they would consider the source of the noise to be any other thing than the passing shadow?

GLAUKON: By Zeus, not me surely.

SOCRATES: Then all in all, would such men not consider reality to be nothing other than the shadows from the passing props?

GLAUKON: Necessarily.

SOCRATES: Consider, then, what would be the condition of someone being released from the chains and their delusion if, as a result of this change, the following scenario would happen to them. When someone would be released and compelled suddenly to stand up and turn their head and walk and look up at the light, as a result he would be distressed and unable, on account of the glittering light of the fire, to see those images which previously he saw as shadows. What do you think he would say if someone said to him that in the past what he saw was nonsense but now he was looking at things nearer to reality and more true since he was turned to more real things? Moreover, if someone, displaying each of the props to him, would force him to answer the question of what it is, do you think that he would be puzzled and consider the shadows he saw earlier to be more true than the props he was now being shown?

GLAUKON: Of course.

SOCRATES: Then, if he was also forced to look at the light itself, would he not feel pain in his eyes and flee, turning back again to the shadows which he was able to see distinctly and consider them to be more clear in regard to reality than the props now shown?

GLAUKON: Of course.

SOCRATES: And if someone should drag him by force from there along the rough and steep ascent and not let him go before he dragged him into the light of the sun, then, would he not, since he was forced like that, be pained and angry? And, since his eyes would be filled with beams of light when he came into the light, would he be able to see the things now being labeled as reality?

GLAUKON: Not immediately, at any rate.

SOCRATES: Would it not take some time if he intended to see the higher reality? As a result, he would more easily perceive shadows, and after this images in the water of men and other things, and later the things themselves. After these stages, he would next see celestial phenomena and the sky itself, looking at the light of the stars and moon more easily at night than at midday, because of the light from the sun.

GLAUKON: Of course.

SOCRATES: Finally, then, he would be able to look upon the sun, not in water or some other reflective surface, but he would be able to see it in its proper place and its core essence and behold it for what it is.

GLAUKON: Indeed.

SOCRATES: After this stage, he would presently conclude that the sun is the provider of the seasons and the years and the governor of all things in the visible region and in some fashion the cause of all those things he was seeing.

GLAUKON: It is clear that these conclusions would surely follow. What then?

SOCRATES: Do you not think that he, after recalling his prior habitation and what was considered wisdom there and his fellow prisoners, would be happy about the change and pity them?

GLAUKON: Very much.

SOCRATES: And if the fellow prisoners bestowed honors and commendations and privileges for the one seeing most swiftly the passing shadows and remembering which shadows were first and last carried across and being most able to announce like a prophet what was to come, do you think that he would desire such honors? Would he be jealous of those being honored by the masses or those exercising dominion, or contrariwise would he agree with the vignette in Homer concerning Achilles, and rather wish a life in lowly servitude, being attached to the soil, alongside a man in poverty and ultimately suffer anything rather than believe that reality to be true and live in that way?

GLAUKON: Yes.

SOCRATES: And indeed consider this as well: if such a man, after coming back down, would sit in his old seat, would not his eyes be full of darkness since he came suddenly from the sunlight? Now, if once more he would be required to contend with the unenlightened prisoners in discerning the shadows, while he is still dim-sighted and before his eyes were restored—and the time for habituation would not be very short—would he not cause laughter, and would it not be said of him that by going up he ruined his eyes and that it is not worth the attempt to go up? And if, by some means, they were able to lay hands on and even kill the one attempting to release and enlighten them, would they not do so.

GLAUKON: Oh, we surely know that.

SOCRATES: Accordingly, dear Glaukon, one must apply this entire allegory to what was said before: firstly, comparing the place revealed through sight to the chamber of the prison and secondly the light of the fire in it to the power of the sun. And if you reckon the ascension and the viewing of the things above to be the way up of the soul into the region of the intellect, you will not miss my belief, since you desire to hear this. But I think only god knows whether this is the truth. In any case my further thoughts appear as follows: the final thing seen, and that with great difficulty, is the idea of the good. Once apprehended, one needs to conclude that this is altogether the cause of all true and beautiful things, giving birth in the visible world to light and the ruling power of light and in the intelligible world the good serves as the ultimate source of truth and mind. Hence, it is imperative for anyone intending to act sensibly, either in private or public affairs, to contemplate the good.

GLAUKON: I concur, at least to the degree I understand.

SOCRATES: Come then and assent to the next point and not find it strange that those who've reached that level are not willing to be busy with the affairs of men, but their souls always hasten to spend time aloft. For I suppose that this is right, if the agreed upon analogy again holds true.

GLAUKON: Certainly, it is likely.

SOCRATES: What about this? Do you think it is at all surprising, if a man, coming from contemplating divine affairs to worthless human affairs, disgraces himself and appears very ridiculous while still dim-sighted and before he became sufficiently habituated to the present darkness? When he is compelled to fight in the courts of law or in some other place, does he not contend about the mere shadows of justice, or other images of which they are copies, and strive earnestly in this endeavor, whenever these matters are taken up by those not knowing justice itself?

GLAUKON: That would hardly be surprising.

SOCRATES: But if someone is sensible, he would remember that the two disturbances in the eyes arise from two sources: by changing from the light to darkness or darkness into light. And, since he also believes these same things happen to the soul, when he sees a soul thrown into confusion and unable to perceive something, he would not laugh thoughtlessly, but he would reflect whether coming from a brighter life the soul is blinded by unfamiliar darkness or coming from full ignorance into greater brightness the soul is filled with flashing brilliance. And indeed, he would consider the one soul blessed on account of its experience and course of life and pity the other. If he wished to laugh at the second soul, his laughter would be less scornful than the laughter at the soul coming from the brilliance above.

GLAUKON: What you are saying is very reasonable.

SOCRATES: Then we must necessarily hold the following opinions about these matters. If they are true, education is not what some men pronounce it to be. For they say that they insert knowledge in the soul which was not there, just like putting sight into blind eyes.

GLAUKON: They do indeed say that.

SOCRATES: But the present argument indicates that this power in the soul of each person is innate and the organ with which each of us understand is just like the eye, in that the eye is not functional without turning the whole body from darkness to the light; in the same way this organ of thought must be turned from the mundane world with the whole soul until the soul becomes able to bear up while gazing upon being itself and the brightest portion of being—and this we call the good, do we not?

GLAUKON: Yes.

SOCRATES: Therefore, there could be an art for this very thing, this rotation, by which the soul is turned most easily and effectually, not for the production of sight in it, because it already has this, but because it is not turned correctly or looking where it should in order to facilitate the necessary learning.

GLAUKON: It certainly seems likely.

Translator's Note

Plato's "Allegory of the Cave," from Book 7 of his *Republic,* is arguably the most famous piece of Western philosophy, and its influence permeates all academic thought in Western culture. Indeed, it is still a staple in introductory philosophy courses today.

The purpose of the allegory is to lay out Plato's conception of what comprises reality. It is the third argument in *The Republic* in a series that attempts this explication. At the end of Book 6 there is the "Simile of the Sun to the Good" (507.a–509.c), "The Divided Line" (509.d–511.e), and the "Allegory of the Cave" in the opening of Book 7 (514.a–520.3). All three arguments propose the same dichotomy of reality.

For Plato, the separating line is between the mundane, visible world of sticks, rocks and chairs and the higher reality of the intellectual realm. Each of these realms can be subdivided into two again, with a gradation of reality.

At the lowest level of the mundane world is where most people are trapped (the prisoners in the allegory). Their level of understanding is conjecture and opinion, as it is based on shadows and reflections (e.g. the shadows on the wall of the cave). The second level of the mundane world is represented by those behind the chained prisoners. While this level is closer to reality than the first, it still falls short. Here we have real objects (the props carried causing the shadows), but knowledge here is still based on belief.

Once the released prisoner is led out of the cave, they have been introduced to the intellectual realm. This is also divided into lower and higher levels of reality. The lower of the two sections is based on understanding through mental calculations with induction and geometry. This stage is represented in the allegory by the beginning experiences out of the cave of reflections in water.

In the final stage, reason dominates and leads the prisoner to deduction and pure ideas. It is the contemplation of abstract ideas, justice, beauty, holiness (Plato's famous forms) that leads to knowledge, truth and reality. The peak experience at this level is the contemplation of "The Good." It is only once one has learned what "The Good" is, that one can act wisely.

Images, then, lead to opinion, objects to belief, and abstract ideas to understanding, and pure ideas to reason. In the remainder of Book 7, Plato lays out the steps involved in the progress that must be attained by the philosopher king.

All of this begs the question, though, whether Plato is correct or not with his analogy.

—DREW MANNATTER, Ph.D.
MARCH 21, 2025

Acknowledgments

Grateful acknowledgement to the editors of the following journals, magazines and anthologies in which these poems or earlier versions of them first appeared:

10,000 Arts: "Hangover, Sunday, 8AM"; *Blackbird:* "Preschool"; *Birmingham Poetry Review:* "The Cave" & "United Martial Arts"; *Copper Nickel:* "Airhose"; *The Cortland Review:* "In the Clearing" & "Good Company"; *New Limestone Review:* "40 Below"; *Northern Grit:* "Duluth"; *Ploughshares:* "Sea Glass"; *Poetry Daily:* "Preschool"; *Terrain.org:* "Trying to Teach My Kids to See Them Coming When I Can't See Them Myself" & "My Daughter Leads Me into The Woods"; *The Southern Review:* "Tick Check" & "Tischer Creek"; *Unsinkable: Poetry Inspired by the Titanic:* "Tischer Creek"

"Orange Sun Rising" appears in the song cycle "Quarantine Camp" by Raphael Fusco after the poems of Ryan Vine, commissioned by The German Forum of New York and published by Ries & Erler Musikverlag of Berlin. The cycle received 2nd Prize from the National Association of Teachers of Singing for the Art Song Competition.

"Trying to Teach My Kids to See Them Coming When I Can't See Them Myself" & "My Daughter Leads Me into the Woods" were 2023 finalists for *Terrian.org*'s annual poetry contest. "Sea Glass" & "The Cave" were longlisted for *Frontier Poetry*'s 2022 Nature and Place Prize. "Air Hose" was longlisted for *Pallet Poetry*'s 2020 Emerging Poet Prize

Thanks to all the amazing artists who've supported this work along the way: Taylor Collier, Raphael Fusco, Erik Tschekunow, Angie Mason, Jennifer Sperry Steinorth, Jason Iwen, Connie Wanek, Patrick Phillips, Mahagony Brown, Barton Sutter, Michael Bazzett and Ilya Kaminski. And thanks to J. Bruce Fuller and the whole TRP team for trusting my work and sending it again into the world.

Thanks Dr. Ashley Comstock and Dr. Drew Mannetter for fielding my questions about Plato and his allegory.

Thanks to The School of Arts and Sciences and English Department of the College of St. Scholastica for the Fall '23 sabbatical, during which the bulk of this book was written, or at least polished.

Thanks to the Minnesota State Arts Board for their continued support.

And thanks Shawna, a thousand thanks!, for putting up with my endless prattle about poetry, but mostly thanks for your profound support. I wouldn't have finished this book without you. Bésame mucho, mi amor.

And thanks Leo & Aili for the abundant, unconditional love. I know much of this book seems sad, but what I'm trying to say is how happy you've made me.

Ryan Vine is a fiscal year 2023 recipient of a Creative Support for Individuals Grant from the Minnesota State Arts Board. This activity is made possible by the voters of Minnesota through a grant from the Minnesota State Arts Board, thanks to a legislative appropriation from the arts and cultural heritage fund.

About the Author

Ryan Vine is the author of *To Keep Him Hidden* (Salmon Poetry, 2018), winner of the Northeastern Minnesota Book Award; and the chapbooks *WARD* (TRP, 2021); and *Distant Engines* (Backwaters Press, 2006), winner of a Weldon Kees Award. His poems have appeared in *The American Poetry Review, Ploughshares, The Rumpus, Blackbird, The Southern Review, Poetry Ireland Review, Poetry Daily, Verse Daily,* and on National Public Radio's *The Writer's Almanac.* He is Professor of English at the College of St. Scholastica in Duluth, MN.

21st Century Poets

21st Century Poets is a collection of full-length poetry books by TRP authors whose first book of poetry was released after the year 2000.

BOOKS IN THIS SERIES

No. 001 — Kendall Dunkelberg—*Time Capsules*

No. 002 — William Bedford Clark—*Blue Norther and Other Poems*

No. 003 — Karla K. Morton—*Names We've Never Known*

No. 004 — Ben Greer—*The Bright House*

No. 005 — Beryl Lawn—*Poems from Both Sides of the Fence*

No. 006 — Swep Lovitt—*Sometimes the World Is Too Beautiful*

No. 007 — William Wright—*Bledsoe*

No. 008 — Sarah Cortez—*Walking Home*

No. 009 — Jesse Graves—*Tennessee Landscape with Blighted Pine*

No. 010 — Richard Boada—*The Error of Nostalgia*

No. 011 — Sarah Cortez—*Cold Blue Steel*

No. 012 — David Havird—*Map Home*

No. 013 — Beryl Lawn—*More Poems from Both Sides of the Fence*

No. 014 — Jesse Graves—*Basin Ghosts*

No. 015 — Karla K. Morton—*A Constant State of Leaping*

No. 016 — Kendall Dunkelberg—*Barrier Island Suite*

No. 017 — Stephen Gibson—*The Garden of Earthly Delights*

No. 018 — Karla K. Morton—*Accidental Origami: New and Selected Works*

No. 019 — Karla K. Morton—*Wooden Lions*

No. 020 — Mary Morris—*Enter Water, Swimmer*

No. 021 — Elisabeth Murawski—*Heiress*

No. 022 — Randall Watson—*The Geometry of Wishes*

No. 023 — Sarah Kain Gutowski—*Fabulous Beast*

No. 024 — Jennifer Sperry Steinorth—*A Wake with Nine Shades*

No. 025 — Mary Morris—*Dear October*

No. 026 — Andrew Hemmert—*Sawgrass Sky*

No. 027 — Matt W. Miller—*Tender the River*

No. 028 — Jesse Graves—*Tennessee Landscape with Blighted Pine* (10th Anniversary Edition)

No. 029 — Forrest Rapier—*As the Den Burns*

No. 030 — Sarah Audsley—*Landlock X*

No. 031 — Luke Johnson—*Quiver*

No. 032 — Sarah Kain Gutowski—*The Familiar*

No. 033 — Joshua Robbins—*Eschatology in Crayon Wax*

No. 034 — Theodora Ziolkowski—*Ghostlit*

No. 035 — Kimberly Ann Priest—*tether & lung*

No. 036 — Mary Morris—*Lanterns in the Night Market*

No. 037 — Daniel Lassell—*Frame Inside a Frame*

No. 038 — Luke Johnson—*Distributary*

No. 039 — Brooke Sahni—*In This Distance*

No. 040 — Randall James Tyrone—*City of Dis*

No. 041 — Ryan Vine—*The Cave*